BUG RIDDLES

Distributed to Schools and Libraries
in Canada by
SAUNDERS BOOK COMPANY
Box 308
Collingwood, Ontario, Canada 69Y3Z7 / (800) 461-9120

Library of Congress Cataloging-in-Publication Data
Woodworth, Viki.
Bug riddles / written & compiled by Viki Woodworth;
illustrated by Viki Woodworth.
p. cm.
Summary: A collection of riddles and jokes about bugs, including
"What sport does a mosquito love? Skin diving."
ISBN 0-89565-864-X
1. Riddles, Juvenile.
[1. Riddles. 2. Jokes. 3. Insects – Wit and humor.] I. Title.
PN6371.W65 1993   91-46671
818′.5402–dc20   CIP / AC

BUG RIDDLES

Compiled and Illustrated by
Viki Woodworth

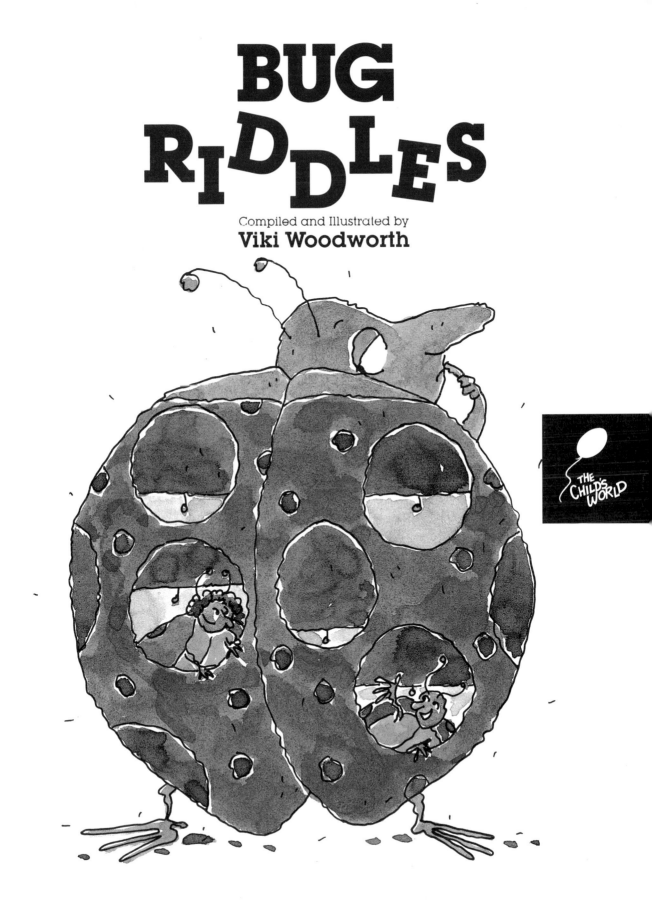

THE CHILD'S WORLD

Why are spiders good storytellers?
They weave a good story, then wind it up at the end.

When two spiders get married, what are they called?
Newly-webs.

Why did the spider go to the doctor?
To find out why it was weaving.

Why did the spider take up knitting?
It was tired of weaving.

How does a spider carry its groceries?
In an egg-sack.

Why does a spider make a good spy?

It knows how to de-bug!

How do a dentist and a carpenter ant fight?
With tooth and nails.

How do termites fight?
They chew each other out.

How do mosquitoes insult each other?
With biting remarks.

How do caterpillars fight?
They walk all over each other.

How do bees insult each other?
With stinging comments.

How do bees call each other?
They give each other a buzz.

Customer: Waiter, there's a fly in my soup!
Waiter: Get it out before it drowns, sir.

Customer: Waiter, there's a singing bug in my soup!
Waiter: Must be a Beatle, sir.

Customer: What's this spider doing in my soup?
Waiter: Looks like he's eating the fly.

Customer: Waiter, why is this giant fly sitting on the rim of my bowl?
Waiter: Because it won't fit *into* the bowl!

Customer: Waiter, this soup is too hot and it has a worm in it!
Waiter: You did order the soup wormed.

Customer: Waiter, there's the biggest fly I've ever seen in my soup!
Waiter: Welcome to Texas.

What happens when a grasshopper drinks coffee?
It feels jumpy.

When is a grasshopper furious?
When it's hopping mad.

What sport does a mosquito love?
Skin diving.

Which bug is losing weight?
The lightning bug.

Which bug is the fastest?
The lightning-quick bug.

Which bug is good to add to your wash?
The whitening bug.

Which bug needs a bath?
The stink bug.

Which bug is handy on a long hike?
The walking stick.

Which bug goes to church regularly?
The praying mantis.

What kind of fly always sounds sick?
The hoarse fly.

Which bug chews tobacco?
The spit bug.

What kind of bugs come from the moon?
Lunar-ticks.

Why did the lady flea look down on the man flea?
She was on a high horse.

What do daredevil fleas do?
Swap horses in midstream.

What do you get when a doctor prescribes lotion to a bug?
A fly in the ointment.

What happens when two flies fight over a cup?
One flies off the handle.

What happens when a lightning bug dives into hot oil?
It's just a flash in the pan.

What do you have when a bug gets stuck in your hat?
A bee in your bonnet.

What type of insect discovers all your secrets?
The worm worms everything out of you.

What kind of worm lived in King Arthur's time?
The knight-crawler.

What do you call an unreliable worm?
A fly-by-night-crawler.

Which end of the worm is the head?
The one with the hat.

What does the inchworm want to be when it grows up?
A footman.

Why should you put worms in your carpet?
It improves the soil.

Where was the beetle when the sun went down?
In the dark.

What's it called when a moth cries?
A moth bawl.

What's the best insect soup?
A moth broth.

When did the moth get sick?
When it ate a polyester sweater.

Why did the moth chase the lightning bug?
Because the moth couldn't read in the dark.

What do you call a big dance for moths?
A moth ball.

What bug is a great bowler?
The boll weevil.

What bug loves math?
The arithmetick.

What's the greasiest bug?
The butter-fly.

What do insects drink?
Bug juice.

What insect club allows only female members?
The ladybug club.

What bug is a good singer?
The hum-bug.

How does an insect keep its hair out of its eyes?
With a hor-net.

How do we know fleas are terrible mothers?
Their children go to the dogs.

What kind of disease do chewing bugs get?
Termitis.

Where do termites read books?
At branch libraries.

How do termites relax?
They take a coffee-table break.

What school does Sherlock Termite attend?
Elementary, of course.

Why did the lady beetle snub the bee?
She thought he was bee-neath her.

What did the mother bee name her middle child?
Bee Tween.

How does a bee comb its hair?
With a honeycomb.

What does a bee do all day?
It keeps buzzy.

What do you get when you cross a bee with a rhinoceros?
I don't know, but I hope it doesn't sting me!

What do you get when you cross a bee with a rabbit?
A honey bunny.

What is the largest ant?
The *Gi*ant.

What bug is handy at a barbecue?
Fire ants.

What do you call the animal that ate Sarah's mother's sister?
An auntie-eater.

What does a nervous carpenter ant do?
Chews nails.

When is a carpenter ant allowed to become a pilot?
When it gets its wings.

Customer: Waiter, why is the fly in my salad?
Waiter: Because you didn't order soup.

Customer: Waiter, there's a crying bug in my soup!
Waiter: Of course he's crying! You just ate his mother.

Customer: Waiter, what is this carpenter ant doing in my soup?
Waiter: Looks like he's building an ark, sir.

Customer: Waiter, why is there a smiling fly in my soup?
Waiter: I think he likes you.

Customer: Waitress, there's a ladybug crying in my soup.
Waitress: Well, give her a handkerchief.

What drives a centipede crazy?
Deciding which shoes to wear.

How many inches will a centipede grow?
Not many inches, but lots of feet.

What did the bad caterpillar say when he was arrested?
I promise I'll turn over a new leaf.

Which bug would have helped Samson hold up the building?
The cater-pillar.

Which bug is the most respectable?
The cater-pillar of society.

What bug has its own food business?
The cater-pillar.